Little Laureates

Gtr Manchester Vol II

Edited by Claire Tupholme

Young**Writers**

First published in Great Britain in 2008 by:
Young Writers
Remus House
Coltsfoot Drive
Peterborough
PE2 9JX
Telephone: 01733 890066
Website: www.youngwriters.co.uk

SB ISBN 978-1 84431 475 1

Foreword

Young Writers was established in 1991 and has been passionately devoted to the promotion of reading and writing in children and young adults ever since. The quest continues today. Young Writers remains as committed to the nurturing of poetic and literary talent as ever.

This year's Young Writers competition has proven as vibrant and dynamic as ever and we are delighted to present a showcase of the best poetry from across the UK and in some cases overseas. Each poem has been selected from a wealth of *Little Laureates* entries before ultimately being published in this, our sixteenth primary school poetry series.

Once again, we have been supremely impressed by the overall quality of the entries we have received. The imagination, energy and creativity which has gone into each young writer's entry made choosing the poems a challenging and often difficult but ultimately hugely rewarding task - the general high standard of the work submitted ensured this opportunity to bring their poetry to a larger appreciative audience.

We sincerely hope you are pleased with this final collection and that you will enjoy *Little Laureates Gtr Manchester Vol II* for many years to come.

Contents

Haashim Ahmed (7)	65
Amaani Esmail (7)	65
Seif Mohammed (8)	66
Amera Hussain (7)	66
Talha Khan (8)	67

St Charles' RC Primary School, Swinton

Joshua Flynn (10)	67
Louise Hawkens (8)	67
Brittany Lowe (10)	68
Joe Gorman (11)	68
Helen Morley (10)	69
Kieron Robert Fawcett (10)	69
Katherine Shanley (10)	70
Daniel Moore (10)	70
Laura Woodward (9)	71
Shaun Taylor-Whitfield (11)	71
Natasha Martland (9)	72
Ryan McGuinness (10)	72
Gemma Johns (10)	73
Deklan Cusick (10)	73
Jason Lineker (10)	74
Molly Frattasi (10)	74
Juliette Graham (7)	74
Joel Healey (10)	75
Beth Renshaw (7)	75
Finlay Cox (7)	75
Joseph McMullen (10)	76
Nicole Greenhalgh (11)	76
Matthew Smith (9)	77
Emily Naylor (7)	77
Jazmine Barker (9)	78
Sebastian Ward-Bowmer (10)	78
Abigail Hamer (9)	79
Matthew Hope (7)	79
Charlie Beth Parker (7)	79
Emma Mollard (10)	80
Lauren Ainscough (8)	80
Olivia Adelaide Myrtle (9)	80
Robert Barton (8)	81
Harry Warburton (9)	81

Maisie Cox (8)	81
Kristine Norwood (9)	82
Chloe Broughall (9)	82
Natalya Cusick (8)	83
Amy Plaister (9)	83
Jack Grimes (8)	83
Georgia Tandy (8)	84
Lukas Copak (8)	84
Melissa Capps (8)	84

St James' CE Primary School, Birch-in-Rusholme

Haniyya Shaikh (9)	85
Harry Joseph Gallagher (9)	86
Alice Hare (9)	86
Laura Clarke (9)	87

St Mary's CE Primary School, Urmston

Esmé Elizabeth Doolin (8)	87

Seedley Primary School

Jodie McRoy (9)	88
Bianca Tadete (9)	89
Sam Curwen (9)	90
Callum James Henderson-Playfair (9)	91
Caitlin Alice Craddock (9)	92
Gemma Wagstaffe (10)	93
Chloe Rawlings (9)	94
Jordan Egerton (9)	95

Temple Primary School

Hamza Tahir (8) & Ahsan Mohsin	95
Shamera Ashfaq (8) & Mevish Ahmed	96
Shoaib Mohammed (8) & Mohammed Hafeez	97
Ifla Araf (8) & Sabah Gohar	97

The Poems

Fear

Fear looks like a big monster coming at you
Fear tastes like out-of-date milk
Fear smells like stinky socks
Fear feels like a dry sponge being squeezed giving you goosebumps.

Alexander Cunningham (8)

The Amazing Great White Shark

The amazing great white shark,
Who lives in the deep blue sea,
Fast, hungry, bloodthirsty,
Like a cheetah under the sea,
Like a bullet from an underwater cannon,
It makes me feel concerned,
Like a diver waiting to discover hidden treasures,
The amazing great white shark,
Reminds us of the saying:
They are more scared of us than we are of them.

Vincent French (10)
Acacias Community Primary School

The Charming Peacock

The charming peacock,
The most appealing of birds,
Dazzling, attractive, phenomenal,
Its feathers are as iridescent as a rainbow,
Its neck is as lengthy as a horse's,
It makes me feel so repulsive,
Like an ogre that has no grace,
The charming peacock,
Reminds us nature is beautiful.

Zahra Lokhandwala (10)
Acacias Community Primary School

The Mighty Lion

The mighty lion,
Ruler of the jungle,
Huge, muscular, dangerous,
As blazing as the sun,
As big as a tiger,
It makes me feel weak,
As weak as a young child,
The mighty lion,
Reminds me how wonderful wildlife is.

Humza Jauhar (10)
Acacias Community Primary School

The Brawny Bald Eagle

The brawny bald eagle,
Sovereign of the skies,
Dangerous, powerful, intense,
As rapid as lightning,
As lethal as fire,
It makes me feel substandard,
Like a diminutive child never noticed,
The sovereign bald eagle,
Appreciate its power.

Hamzah Khanzada (10)
Acacias Community Primary School

Happiness

Happiness is gold like the sun
It smells like red roses
It tastes like berries
It looks like pink roses falling
It feels like smooth rocks
It reminds me of my mum.

Andre Ellison Graham (7)
Acacias Community Primary School

The Crocodile

The vicious crocodile,
A fast swimmer,
Powerful, predatory, proud,
Teeth as sharp as a blade,
As deadly as a dagger,
It makes me feel scared,
It makes me feel like a mouse against a cat,
The vicious crocodile,
A very hungry monster.

Jonathan Stansfield (10)
Acacias Community Primary School

The Great King Tut

The great King Tut,
Lived over two thousand years ago,
Brave, smart, courageous,
He was like a god to the Egyptians,
It makes me feel like nothing,
Like nobody wants to know me,
The great King Tut,
Reminds us of how we are nothing compared to God.

Qasim Yousaf Hussain (10)
Acacias Community Primary School

My Birthdays

My birthday is the 24th of December,
Jolly, caring, sharing,
As colourful as a rainbow,
As white as a clean sheet of paper,
So excited that I could jump to the moon,
My birthdays,
How lucky I am to have such a brilliant birthday.

Jacob Oliver Hand (10)
Acacias Community Primary School

Peregrine Falcon

The amazing peregrine falcon,
The fastest bird of prey,
Beautiful, amazing, graceful,
As fast as a rocket,
As deadly as a torpedo,
Makes me feel slow,
Like a pensioner on a Zimmer frame,
The amazing peregrine falcon,
Reminds us what speed is.

Cairo Lewis (10)
Acacias Community Primary School

The Mighty Cobra

The mighty slithering cobra,
The most dangerous snake alive,
Powerful, mighty, long,
Like the size of a tree,
Like a tongue pointing to Heaven,
It makes me feel tiny,
Like a minute ant,
The great cobra,
Reminds us how long our life is.

Saqib Mahmood (10)
Acacias Community Primary School

Love

Love is like red, nice-smelling roses
Love sounds like a bee buzzing
It smells like fresh air
It tastes like a sweet Love Heart
It looks like delicious chocolate
Love feels like a giant snowflake
It reminds me of going on holiday.

Uzma Shaikh (7)
Acacias Community Primary School

The Great White Shark

The great white shark,
It's got razor-sharp teeth,
Mighty, bloodthirsty, fearsome,
Like a cheetah jumping out for its prey,
Like a tiger ripping apart some flesh,
It makes me feel like I'm going to get torn apart,
But the great white shark,
It makes me feel that I'm the weakest thing in the world,
The great white shark,
It reminds me of how powerful the great white shark is.

Musab Navid (10)
Acacias Community Primary School

Fear

Fear is red like the burning hot sun
It sounds like a grey volcano
It smells like a smelly bear's foot
It tastes like a red-hot rose
It looks like a fat old sausage
It feels like terrible hot lava
It reminds me of a nightmare.

Dhaniyah Jauhar (7)
Acacias Community Primary School

Love

Love is pink like a pretty rose
It sounds like beautiful birds singing
It smells like dark chocolate
It tastes like sweet candyfloss
It looks like a fun thing to do
It feels like white snow falling
It reminds me of surfing with my family.

Jaidah Hanley (7)
Acacias Community Primary School

The Deadly Cheetah

The deadly cheetah,
Fastest land animal,
Mighty, powerful, dangerous,
Like a bullet fired at its prey,
Like lightning dashing down to Earth,
It makes me feel slow,
As slow as a snail,
Reminds us how amazing creatures can be.

Zuraiz Choudhary (10)
Acacias Community Primary School

Sadness

Sadness is black like a witch's hat
It sounds like a baby crying
It smells like damp water
It tastes like black coffee
It looks like dark worms
It feels like you are scared
It reminds me of a scared animal.

Anisa Jabbar (7)
Acacias Community Primary School

Anger

Anger is red like exploding fire
It sounds like a lion's mighty roar
It smells like burning hot lava
It tastes like spicy chilli
It looks like the red-hot sun
It feels like a volcano erupting
It reminds me of lava and fire.

Luke Stansfield (7)
Acacias Community Primary School

The Colourful Rainbow

The colourful rainbow,
Has all the colours you can think of,
Magical, beautiful, amazing,
Like a pathway to Heaven,
Like a sparkling slide to the unknown,
When I see a rainbow, I feel a sparkling sensation inside me,
The colourful rainbow,
It makes me feel as if I'm walking on the clouds.

Heather Oakes (10)
Acacias Community Primary School

Love

Love is red like a lovely smelling rose
It sounds like music that is romantic
It smells like the air in the countryside
It tastes like dark chocolate ice cream
It looks like a dark red balloon floating into the sky
It feels like a soft white mattress
It reminds me of orange cheese on toast.

Matthew Hines (7)
Acacias Community Primary School

Happiness

Happiness is yellow like the burning sun
It smells like a beautiful rose
It tastes like apple juice
It looks like beautiful flowers
It feels like nice grass
It reminds me of my family.

Seiful Islam (7)
Acacias Community Primary School

Happiness

Happiness is pink like lots of roses
It sounds like good freedom
It smells like a very nice day outside
It tastes like wonderful chocolate
It looks like big fun
It feels like very good love
It reminds me of when I first met Andre.

Malachi Chinery (7)
Acacias Community Primary School

Fear

Fear is black like the dark night
It sounds like a screaming sound
It smells like burning hot toast
It tastes like a rotten sandwich
It looks like a roaring, scary tiger
It feels like you're in a haunted house
It reminds me of a ghost.

Rafia Khanum (7)
Acacias Community Primary School

Fear

Fear is grey like a grey diamond
Fear smells like hot sweat
Fear looks like the hot sun
Fear tastes like burning blood
Fear sounds like a creaking docr
Fear feels like fighting
Fear reminds me of a scary house.

Amina Nazir (7)
Acacias Community Primary School

Anger

Anger is red like a volcano just about to erupt
It sounds like an earthquake rumbling
It smells like smoke in a car's engine
It tastes like a sizzling barbecue
It looks like a red plant growing
It feels like burning flames
It reminds me of traffic lights that say stop.

Taj Lewis Edwards (7)
Acacias Community Primary School

Fear

Fear is red like a burning tree
It sounds like a growling bear
It smells like an erupting volcano
It tastes like a sizzling sausage
It looks like a red bull coming towards me
It feels like lava burning my hand
It reminds me of a bee stinging me.

James Ballinger (7)
Acacias Community Primary School

Happiness

Happiness is yellow like the shining sun
It sounds like everyone laughing
It smells like the sun shining
It tastes like cherries
It looks like everybody smiling
It feels like you have lots of friends
It reminds me of my dad playing with me.

Alishan Khan (7)
Acacias Community Primary School

Love

Love is pink like a flamingo's skin
It sounds like music to my ears
It smells like the air of freedom
It tastes like pink, light candyfloss
It looks like the breeze in the sky
It feels like a soft, cosy blanket
It reminds me of angels in the snow.

Saaqib Fahid (7)
Acacias Community Primary School

Anger

Anger is red like a ripe strawberry
It sounds like an erupting volcano
It smells like burning hot lava
It tastes like a mouldy sandwich
It looks like a small bunch of roses
It feels like burnt toast
It reminds me of arguments.

Amal Naqvi (7)
Acacias Community Primary School

Love

Love is pink like little roses
It sounds like birds singing in the treetops
It smells like freedom in the air
It tastes like crunchy candyfloss
It looks like flowers and stars in the sky
It feels like the clouds are coming down
It reminds me of when I made my snowman.

Paige Jones-Forth (7)
Acacias Community Primary School

Sadness

Sadness is yellow
It sounds like a big animal
It smells like burnt grass
It tastes like a crocodile's claw
It looks like a dark forest
It feels like some sweaty socks
It reminds me of a baby crying.

Haleema Afzal (7)
Acacias Community Primary School

Fear

Fear is grey like a thunderstorm
It sounds like someone shaking
It smells like burning ashes
It tastes like blood
It looks like a ghost going through a door
It feels like you want to cry
It reminds me of going on a roller coaster.

Ruby Jennison (7)
Acacias Community Primary School

Happiness

Happiness is glimmering gold in the sunlight
It sounds like an angel calling from above
It smells like fresh air
It tastes like fresh cherries
It looks like the deep blue sea
It feels like soft sand
It reminds me of smiley faces.

Niall Hurley (7)
Acacias Community Primary School

Cats

Cats are cute,
Cats are lazy,
When cats eat catnip,
Cats go crazy.

Cats are sweet,
Cats like eating cat food,
If you pull a cat's tail,
Cats go in a mood.

Cats are colourful,
Cats have paws,
Cats have pointy ears,
Cats don't have to follow laws.

Cats are my favourite animal,
Cats are great to me,
I've got a cat, you know,
Her name's Millie.

Megan Booth (9)
Acacias Community Primary School

The Rainbow

The rainbow,
When the sun reflects on the rain,
Stunning, soaring, beautiful,
Like an explosion of colour,
Like a bridge to happiness,
It makes me feel safe,
Like a tiny light of hope,
The rainbow,
It reminds me of all the wonderful things in life.

Kiera Bell (10)
Acacias Community Primary School

The Doctor

The Doctor's very keen
To battle a Slitheen
He really likes to stop
An Abzorbaloff
He stays out till half-ten
Battling Cybermen
He has a friend called Rose
Who keeps him on his toes
He also met some Ood
Who made some horrible food
It's a good job they didn't add any garlic
It might have attracted a Dalek
He met a man called The Master
Who tried to make the TARDIS go faster
But at the end of the day
He wants to return home to Gallifrey.

Ruby Sacofsky (10)
Acacias Community Primary School

Happiness

Happy, happy, happy!
I am so happy!
These are the things that make me happy:
Happiness is a sky, azure blue, like in California
Do you like blue skies?
Happiness is the sun setting on the blue sea
Happiness is when my birthday comes
That I have to put up my thumbs
When my birthday comes
Happy, happy, happy!
That is what makes me happy
What makes you happy?

Olivia Mills (9)
Acacias Community Primary School

Happiness

Happiness is colourful flowers like pink, yellow, green and blue
Happiness is seeing a beautiful rainbow in the blue sky
I am happy when there is no school, yes!
Happiness is playing with my friends
Happiness is singing at my school
Happiness is a newborn puppy
Happiness is when you get all the class merits
Happiness is going to a fair
Happiness is watching TV
Happiness is dancing
Happiness is having a little sister
Happiness is reading.

Ellis Benjamin (9)
Acacias Community Primary School

Fear

Fear is the colour of a rosy-red apple
It sounds like someone creeping up on me
It smells like burning fire
It tastes like salt from a tear in my mouth
It feels like freezing cold snow
It reminds me of tiny, slimy creatures on my spine.

Mariam Dar (7)
Acacias Community Primary School

Happiness

Happiness is the Son of God,
Happiness is me being a captain in rugby and scoring lots of tries,
Happiness is me winning the championship in football,
Yes! What a goal!
Happiness is me playing with my dogs Monty and Jessie in the field.

Daniel Dunn (9)
Acacias Community Primary School

Happiness

Happiness is like a bunch of multicoloured flowers
Growing on a nice, hot day
Happiness is waking up on Christmas Day with lots of snow falling
Out of the dark, grey, colourless sky
Tick-tock, tick-tock as the day goes on, the more happiness I get
Happiness is like when I see a dolphin diving in the dark blue sea
Happiness is like a double Flake ice cream that will never ever melt!
What makes you happy?

Daniel Pennington (10)
Acacias Community Primary School

Happiness

Happiness is the word that makes me smile,
Happiness is the word which makes me flow just like the River Nile,
Happiness is the world you want without sadness,
It's about celebration and joy,
Happiness is the life we all want,
Happiness are the smiles that are inside you all along
And the smiles and the laughter are inside you all the time.

Awais Ahmed (10)
Acacias Community Primary School

Happiness

Happiness is when I see a group of dolphins in the deep blue sea
Happiness is a drive in the countryside under a gorgeous blue sky
Happiness is eating fish fingers with my family!
Happiness is watching TV with my family
Happiness is playing on my Game Boy or Nintendo DS
Happiness is eating my curry in the morning
Happiness is looking at animals.

Aaron Flowers-Blades (9)
Acacias Community Primary School

Happiness

I am happy like a cheery bunny
Nobody can stop me being funny
Puppies make me happy 'cause they are funny and strange
But sometimes they can be little pains!
Though I still think puppies are the best
They've got lovely, brown, shiny fur
Tick-tock, tick-tock!
It's time to play!
Don't worry, we will have a good day!
I love pasta and pork, you know I will eat it today
Oh, that reminds me, I was having it anyway!
I love going on holiday on a plane
Do you like going on holiday?
I love Greece and Lanzarote
Have you been to those places?

Rachel Massey (9)
Acacias Community Primary School

The Witches' Spell

(Based on 'Macbeth' by William Shakespeare)

'Double, double, toil and trouble,
Fire burn and cauldron bubble.'
Tail of cat and tongue of frog,
Intestines of rat and blood of teacher,
Head of mouse and foot of anteater,
Tooth of shark and fin of whale,
Paw of hyena and head of male,
Guts of rhino and leg of spider,
Antler of gazelle and fur of tiger,
Heart of boy and mane of unicorn,
Brain of fish and leg of fawn.
'Double, double, toil and trouble,
Fire burn and cauldron bubble.'

Maren Fulton (8)
Acacias Community Primary School

Happiness

Happiness is celebrating Eid
Happiness is a big basket of flowers
Red, green, yellow, blue, pink and purple
Happiness is going out with my friends
Playing tig, football, basketball, netball, swimming and cycling
Happiness is the yellow sun, like hot, blazing sand
Happiness is winning prizes, cards, pencils, marbles
Football cards, cars and badges
Happiness is staying at home watching TV
Lots of cartoons on TV
Happiness is working at school
And watching the blue and white sky
Happiness is having a colourful, beautiful ice cream
Happiness is going on the beach
And playing in the blue, glassy sea with the wind in my face
Happiness is helping people get on in school
And helping them learn stuff
Happiness is . . . what do you think?

Naima Ghuri (9)
Acacias Community Primary School

Happiness

Happiness is a lovely, colourful rainbow in a gleaming blue sky
On a fresh summer's day
Happiness is having a sweet, sweet ice cream
Happiness shows I love my mum and dad
Happiness is looking at fresh flowers on a lovely day
Happiness is going on holiday for free
Happiness is reading happy books by myself
Happiness is playing outside basketball with my friends
Happiness is playing together
Happiness is eating carrots
Happiness is learning new things
Happiness is riding my bike.

Anzil Rafiq (9)
Acacias Community Primary School

The Witches' Spell

(Based on 'Macbeth' by William Shakespeare)

'Double, double, toil and trouble,
Fire burn and cauldron bubble.'
Teeth of shark and legs of spider,
Brain of teacher and heart of tiger.
Eye of newt and toe of frog,
Hump of camel and tongue of dog.
Wing of owlet and fur of wolf,
Adder's fork and nose of Rudolph.
Fin of fish and head of mole,
Fillet of snake and dead man's soul.
Guts of rat and blood of bear,
Mane of lion and ear of hare.
Trunk of elephant and smell of skunk,
Stripes of zebra and hand of monk.
Leg of lizard and udder of cow,
Brain of beaver and man's eyebrow.
'Double, double, toil and trouble,
Fire burn and cauldron bubble.'

Muttaqee Dar (9)
Acacias Community Primary School

Laughter

When the sea ebbs and flows
Crashing against the rocks
Moaning and screeching for help
I cry
But when the sea is jumping about
I think I hear it laugh
So I laugh with it.

Bradley Tong (11)
Barton Clough Primary School

Do You See What I See When I See The Sea?

I love the way the sea ebbs and flows
As the water goes through me
Tickling my toes

I love the way the sea is calm and serene
As I look out into the horizon
As it sparkles and gleams

I love the sea's colour of sapphire blue
Emerald green and turquoise too

The sea's wail is like children in pain
But I love to hear it again

I love the sea's waves as they crash into the rocks
Then, as it drips back down, like the ticking of the clocks
When you see the horizon it makes you think
As if you were in the Titanic and about to sink

I love the fear and rage of the sea
It makes me think how rough it can be
And that's why I love the sea
It's like just the horizon and me

And that is why the sea is so great
And why it is my best mate
With all of the sea's motion
It's like just one big commotion.

Iman Hamadi (10)
Barton Clough Primary School

The Shimmering Sea

The shimmering sea is a cheerful place to be,
It's a relaxing place just for you and me,
Watching the waves showing their motion,
The foam is like a fantastic potion.

The shimmering sea is a cheerful place to be,
It's a relaxing place just for you and me.

The sea is like a gigantic hand,
The crashing waves are the beat from a band,
The swirling sea is a confusing maze,
It's sparkling and shimmering with the sun's rays.

The shimmering sea is a cheerful place to be,
It's a relaxing place just for you and me.

I feel the sea between my toes,
I watch the wave as it flows,
The shining sea is a diamanté blue,
Do you like the sea too?

The shimmering sea is a cheerful place to be,
It's a relaxing place just for you and me.

Sophie Wood (11)
Barton Clough Primary School

I Love The Sea

I love the sea
With its foamy current
It's peaceful and solitary
I love the sea
Its sapphire waves
Are the centre of my soul
The glossy jewelled current
Is the reason my heart beats
I love the beautiful sea.

Katie Holloway (10)
Barton Clough Primary School

Pool Of Death

Oh, cruel sea, the marshal of the deep
You take souls as I weep.
Oh, cruel sea, take pity on me
Hell is the afterlife and you are the key.
Oh, cruel sea, you are the gun of the Earth
Over blood you shall surf.

Oh, cruel sea, you rushing reaper
When I see you I can only whimper.
Oh, cruel sea, you are as cold as the sand
You take my soul with your evil hand.
Oh, cruel sea, you are the Devil's pet
You are the man I wished I'd never met.

Oh, cruel sea, you roaring beast
You shall slay us from west to east.
Oh, cruel sea, you murderous land
You shall spill blood on the sand.
Oh, cruel sea, you are as dark as death
I say this in my final breath.

Christopher Doherty-Crabtree (10)
Barton Clough Primary School

The Ocean

Sapphire with calm waves
Swooping side to side
With a chilled breeze
The ocean is a light
Under the water
Quiet and relaxed
The ocean is a rough, exciting aqua
Which crashes against the rocks
The ocean has fears full of waves
The ocean is a diamond
Which shines and gleams all day.

Michael Illman (10)
Barton Clough Primary School

Sea Poem

The sea is a relaxing place to be
Just for you and me
The clear, blue, emerald sea
Is the right place for me
I love this beautiful sea
Running up to me
As it sparkles this is something
I want to be
As I watch it go up and down
Far away from a dusty town

The sea is a relaxing place to be
Just for you and me
I love this dazzling sea
And it's all for me
I wish it would stay with me
Until I am free.

Imogen Harris-Hughes (10)
Barton Clough Primary School

The Sea And Me

The sea is a cold place
And the clear blue water shows your face
The sea is a warm hand
It grabs hold of the cold sand

Fishermen can see the charging waves
And the water looks like a million slaves
I stand alone by the sea
Talking to a palm tree

The sea sounds like a crying baby
Plus a dying mermaid lady
The waves look like a glass of water
And they look like Poseidon's daughter.

Adam Joseph Sadler (10)
Barton Clough Primary School

My Dazzling Sea

The sea is like a diamond blue
Even when I am with you
I watch it flow up and ebb down
Far, far away from a dusty town.

The sand is so warm
When the sun rises at dawn
Me and you walking along by the tranquil sea
It's the best place to be
H_2O light glows in my face
Even if my dog has a race.

I love the dancing sea
It's just the place for Mr Henry
I am happy and glad
Not even sad or bad
I love the emerald sea
Oh! I love the sea
Please agree with me!

Kimberley Ellis (10)
Barton Clough Primary School

The Sea And Me

The sea is a cold hand
It grabs hold of the warm sand
The sea is a cold place
And the clear blue water shows your face

Fishermen can hear the siren
The king of the sea is called Poseidon
Fish swim among the waves
Sea urchins hiding in little caves

I stand along by the sea
Talking to a palm tree
My mind is set to the rhythm of the sea
My body is alone, just to be free.

Joshua James Steel (10)
Barton Clough Primary School

The Sea

I stand alone by the sea
And let my imagination run free
The sea is the best place you could be
Why cannot many people see?

The sea is like a kingdom of jewels
It is like a million pools
The waves are galloping horses
And the same as water forces

The sea is coming and grabbing the sand
It looks like a massive hand
The sea is a very lost soul
It is always on the massive role

The sea is a shimmering rug
Lying there, with no one to hug
The sea is a swaying motion
The water is a blue potion

The sea is a place of peace
It is like being in Greece
Not so easy to trip
In its masses it's easy to slip

The sea is a gorgeous sight
And it will not fight
The shimmering sea catches my eye
So I don't want to say, 'Goodbye'

I will stay a bit longer
But I want to see a song.

Isher Rattan (10)
Barton Clough Primary School

The Sparkling Sea And Ocean

I stand alone by the sea
The relaxed atmosphere consoles me
Shades of aqua and icy blue
Put me in a dreamy mood.

She's not always calm
Sometimes she does harm
She moans and groans
Thrashing against the huge grey stones.

Against the sand gently lapping
But when angry, quietly slapping
The sapphire ocean is a blue, melted jewel
A lovely, turquoise-blue pool.

Wailing like a banshee screaming
The salty air sends me dreaming
You are my friend, Ocean.

Reaching out to hug the sand
Like a giant, deep green hand
The quiet, tranquil entering my soul
Rippling and glossy, round you roll.

The foaming blue aurora
Fills me with euphoria
A lovely, beaming shimmer ray
As I watch from the bay.

You are so important to me
I love you, Ocean and Sea.

Hannah Khan (10)
Barton Clough Primary School

The Beautiful Sea

I can hear the beautiful sea,
The tide running in at me,
It drifts from left to right,
It's such a gorgeous sight.

Waves rushing in like a giant hand,
Taking in the lovely golden sand,
As I walk along the shore,
It keeps on coming, more and more.

The lapping waves make me calm,
They keep me away from all harm,
Around me the sea swirl starts to envelop,
Ideas in my mind soon begin to develop.

The waves get bigger during the day,
So danger comes and people can't stay,
The sea gets fierce every night,
Especially when there's a storm in sight.

The amazing turquoise sapphire aurora,
Creates such an enjoyable euphoria.

The shimmering sea catches my eye,
So I never want to say goodbye,
The green, the turquoise and the blue,
They remind me all about you.

Colin Slater (10)
Barton Clough Primary School

The Night Blue Sea

The midnight blue sea
A place for you and me
The sea is a wonderful place to be
Oh! I love the sea

The sea is like a giant hand
Reaching out to get the sand
The sea is a wonderful place to be
Oh! I love the sea

The dolphins jump up and down
And the sea rolls and swishes all round and round

Diamond blue - emerald green
It makes the sea look really mean
Washing up at my toes
Squirting like a hose

The sea is a wonderful place to be
Oh! I love the sea

The shimmering sea motion
Is like a great shimmering potion
I love the shades of icy blue
I love the sea - do you?

Latiya Jennifer Shirley (10)
Barton Clough Primary School

The Ocean

Go for a paddle
Go for a swim or a dip
Creeping so slowly
Watch that you don't slip!

Oh! So - quiet and peaceful
This shimmering blue diamond-like ocean
Rocking so slowly
Bubbling away like a magic potion

The foamy white horses
Galloping through the surging waves
They're frothy, foaming and white capped
A clear blue glaze

The crystalline sapphire waves
Glitter in the sun
Shining so brightly
What glorious fun!

At the bottom of my ocean
The kingdom of jewels is around me lay
Gleaming in the aqua waves
There's no reason to delay!

Sophie Singleton (11)
Barton Clough Primary School

How I See My Sea

I stand alone by the sea
Trying to find the rest of me
The sea flowing up and ebbing down
Messing around, like a clown

Rolling, rising, up it goes
Just watch it while it flows
Blue and green
Sets the scene

Charging its way around
Divers never touch the ground
My mind flows with it and sets free
This is the only place to be

The sea is now very gentle and calm
Softly as you touch its shimmering but soft palm
The spreading waves rustle, like a fresh aqua duvet

This is the first time we meet
Drop, drip
I'm taking a dip
Under the ocean floor
Surging through the blue water with a roar!

Olivia Mae Queeley (11)
Barton Clough Primary School

The Sea

The sea, the sea, beautiful sea,
I love the sound of the sea, it's calling me.
All different colours, turquoise and blue,
It's such a wonderful, lovely view.

The scent of the sea just fills me so much,
As I get hold of the tiny blue diamonds in my clutch.
The waves of the sea creates an aqua hand,
Trying to reach the magnificent, golden sand.

The shimmering sea just catches my eye,
I could watch it all day with a happy sigh.
It is nearly the end of this beautiful day,
Goodbye lovely sea, until next time, I say.

Stephen Zhang (11)
Barton Clough Primary School

Hallowe'en

Scary monsters lurk in darkness
Hunting for green slimy food
Their claws are as sharp as blades of steel
They like their people when they're stewed.

Wizards cast black, smoky spells
Turning people into toads
Witches fly upon a broomstick
Hovering above forbidden roads.

Headless horsemen with pumpkin heads
Riding on skeletal horses
Galloping across marshy land
Wild winds blowing with strong forces.

If you are out on Hallowe'en
Beware of ghosts and ghouls around you
If you catch a glimpse of one
Please be careful what you do!

Samuel Carson (9)
Branwood Prep School

One Day . . .

One day I walked outside,
I looked and I saw a butterfly,
    It was yellow and brown,
It looked a bit like a clown,
    Oh, I like that butterfly!

I turned and looked in the corner,
    There was a squirrel hopping around,
With his bushy tail, lovely and grey,
    I want to snuggle it all day,
The squirrel was carrying a nut around,
    The nut was round and brown.

I turned round, I heard a sound,
    There was a cat saying, *'Miaow! Miaow!'*
I stroked the cat, then went inside to get my hat,
    I put my hat on the cat
And again, the cat miaowed.

Grace MacLennan (11)
Branwood Prep School

Autumn

The leaves in autumn swirl round and round,
    Dancing and prancing, going up and down.
They leap to one side and fall all around,
    Landing in a big, colourful crowd.

Once the trees are finally bare
    And the leaves aren't flying everywhere,
You can jump up and down and hear a loud *crunch!*
    Like tucking into my father's Sunday lunch.

The breeze is cold as the bare branches sway,
    So I run until the leaves fly away.
This carries on, but the days, on, they crawl,
    Until it is time to say goodbye to the wondrous fall.

Natalie Wynn (11)
Branwood Prep School

Mr Nobody

He's the one who leaves his clothes,
In a pile on the bathroom floor.
'Who's left the CDs out of their cases?'
We have a think, but we're not sure.
Maybe it's the same person who lost
The remote control on the settee,
We don't know who's done all this,
Maybe it's that guy, Mr Nobody?

Charlotte Norbury (9)
Branwood Prep School

The Sun

When I am outside playing in the light
I sometimes stop and wonder why it is so bright?
I look into the sky and there is a yellow ball
And so I always think, *why don't you fall*?
When I go to bed, it sometimes is still there
So I lie there and start to stare
It is a fireball in the sky
And then I close my eyes and say goodbye.

David Deer (10)
Branwood Prep School

Mr Nobody

Who left the landing light switched on?
Whoever can it be?
The tap that drips and fills the sink
Am I sure it is not me?
Toys left out on the bedroom floor,
Who played with them last? Me?
Oh, please tell me who it can be?
Is it Mr Nobody?

Brearnna Close (9)
Branwood Prep School

Mr Nobody

He smashes all the wine glasses
He throws his shoes about
He leaves out all the evidence
He's bound to get found out!
Who is this mysterious man?
It must be somebody?
But when you asked who did it though
'Twas Mr Nobody!

Jessica Amy Norbury (9)
Branwood Prep School

Mr Nobody

The toys are lying on the floor,
They're never in the box.
He doesn't ever tidy his room,
It's full of smelly socks!
Outside, the trampoline is dirty and wet,
Yes, we can all agree,
He's left the cover off yet again,
That Mr Nobody!

Lucy Jones (9)
Branwood Prep School

Fast Food

Burgers, crisps and chips
Make me lick my lips,
Chocolate, sweets and lollies
Are always in my trolleys,
Fizzy Fanta and lemonade,
I will never trade,
They are all my favourite foods,
They put me in better moods.

Eve Peden (10)
Branwood Prep School

Rain

Rain is wet
And is cold,
It could be dirty,
It could be clean,
No, it is not cheerful.

Rain is miserable
And will ruin your bikes,
It spoils a day,
Nobody can stand it.

Ravenous rain,
As ragged as a bear,
In a house, it's OK,
Not outside.

Ragged rain,
A car protects you,
If you don't run now,
No, you won't be dry.

Michael Kalra (10)
Branwood Prep School

The Police Box

One day, I saw a police box
And then it looked at me,
I was astonished, very astonished,
It was an amazing sight to see!

The next day I went to the police box,
But this time I went inside,
I saw the inside, it was big, it was marvellous,
It was an astonishing sight to see!

William Henry Welbon (10)
Branwood Prep School

Autumn Leaves

As summer fades away from us, autumn begins,
In two months time, the birds will soon sing,
But now autumn time will soon bring,
Fog and wind, instead of sunshine and breezes
And instead of warming, the sky soon freezes,
Lots and lots of snow coming soon,
Now I have to say goodbye and good afternoon.

Oliver Lambley (10)
Branwood Prep School

Zingy Zaina

I'm as delightful as blossom
And I'm as adorable as a bunny,
Nothing stops me from being as lovely as Miss Katergi,
My brothers are as irritating as a crying baby,
My mum is as pleasant as a beautiful lake,
My dad is as good looking as a pandan,
My friends are as gorgeous as roses,
Often I actually relish Miss Katergi teaching me,
I don't like being untidy.

Zaina Ali (8)
Cheetham Community Primary School

Petite Imaan

I'm as petite as a mouse
Even though I'm the third eldest in my family
Sometimes my sister is a cry baby
But then after a while, she becomes cute
I have black hair
I'm brainy and bright like my dad
I liked going to my uncle's wedding
Because it had entertainment.

Imaan Fazil (8)
Cheetham Community Primary School

Silly Sabah

Although I look gorgeous,
I am still miniature,
I'm clever and intelligent
And a sporty person,
Even though I'm amazing,
I think I'm really witty,
I am as skinny as a lush green plant,
Most people call me Silly Sabah,
I think they're right,
Because I am quite silly,
I know I'm a clever clog,
But not like a barking dog.

In spite of my family being stuck at home,
I'd rather take them to visit the Lord,
Even though my migi sister is miniature,
She goes on interesting adventures,
I have an extremely funny family,
My family is as cheeky as a monkey,
Sometimes I like going swimming,
But most of the time I feel cold,
I really hate meatballs,
But I love Miss Katergi when she smiles!

Sabah Iqbal (8)
Cheetham Community Primary School

Musical Mohammed

I'm as brainy as Mr Barnes
I'm enormously thoughtful
My brother is as disgusting and as horrible as vegetables
My sister is as gorgeous as a flower
I adore reading books
I don't like skipping
My hobbies are football, cricket and the Quran
My hobbies are playing video games.

Mohammed Ali Shan (8)
Cheetham Community Primary School

Oblivious Omamah

I'm as skinny as a stick
And I'm so not thick,
Although I look really nice,
I'm as small as mice,
I'm really, really cool
And I really hate school.

I really think I'm an intelligent clever dog,
But my sister thinks I'm a dumb dog,
I think I'm as speedy as someone that's athletic,
But my sister just takes the mick,
Although, I think I'm as hilarious as clowns,
When I do a cool trick my sister just frowns,
I think my sister's just jealous.

I like to catch fishes,
But I hate to clean the dishes,
I've got a really funny friend
And I think our friendship will never end!

Omamah Choudry (8)
Cheetham Community Primary School

Kind Kanwal

I am as tall as a tree
However, I am speedy like a hamster
Although my hair is long, I like plaiting my hair
However, my eyes are dark brown
Although my brother is 14 years old
He is hilarious and kind
However my cousins are cute even though they don't fight
I love pizza although I don't like mash
Although I dislike beans and spiders
My hobbies are listening to the teacher
And eating my nails.

Kanwal Nawaz (8)
Cheetham Community Primary School

Marvellous Madjda

Although I look very tall,
I've got no chance in basketball,
Even though I'm intelligent at work,
I still find it difficult to concentrate,
I'm as calm as a ladybird,
But sometimes I lose my temper,
I'm very talkative.

I've got a magic mum,
Besides my family is a funny family,
In addition, my family is bright,
My gran is getting on in age,
My sister is impatient,
My older sister's entered secondary school,
So she'll have to study harder.

One of by hobbies is cool chess,
Although the finest sport is swimming
I like super studying,
It's higher quality than the rest,
I'm as sporty as an athlete
Another thing is that I like school
The teachers are useful
But I dislike basketball,
Eventually there is tremendous tennis,
Also hilarious crazy cricket.

Madjda Bougherira (8)
Cheetham Community Primary School

Autumn

Autumn is cold
And shiny brown conkers drop from rusty trees
And when I step on the leaves
They crunch into pieces
The leaves drop onto the ground gently.

Anisa Zahid Fazil (10)
Cheetham Community Primary School

Patient Putri

Although I'm patient,
I still have an enormous heart,
I'm as helpful as a servant,
I'm as delightful as a beautiful queen.

In addition, my brother is so irresponsible
And my toddler is so lovely,
My dad is so charming, pleasing and pleasant,
My mum is loving and caring
And her loveliness is magnificent.

Another thing, I love pizza and I like toys,
The toys are a pleasure,
I love happiness and I like scrumptious ice cream cake
And I appreciate a recent computer,
I don't appreciate running!

Putri Reduan (8)
Cheetham Community Primary School

Helpful Hassan

Although I'm as tall as a tree
I'm still only eight years old
I have very small and dark hair
I am as speedy as a cheetah
Sometimes I can be a lazy ladybird.

My family is very bubbly
My sister is as annoying as a monkey
My baby brother babbles a lot
My sister is sometimes temperamental.

I love football
I abhor avocado
I think this about football - fantastic football
I love chocolate cake.

Hassan Islam (8)
Cheetham Community Primary School

Beautiful Bushra

Although I'm beautiful
I've still got an immense heart
I'm as pretty as a rose
I'm like a daffodil too
Even though I'm the middle one in my family

My dad is as witty as a hyena
However, my sister is as brainy as a doctor
My mum is a fantastic cooker
My other sister is a fat cat

I actually idolise Miss Katergi
I think she looks like a gorgeous rose
I think Miss Katergi is helpful and elegant
My hobby is learning and teaching
My teacher is called Miss Katergi
And is like rising sun shining.

Bushra Khan (8)
Cheetham Community Primary School

Mysterious Maha

Although I'm miniature in size
I'm still as cheeky as a monkey
Often I'm very bubbly
Nothing stops me being as sneaky as a sneak

My sisters are as irritating as a crying baby
My brothers are as sporty as David Beckham
My mum is as bonnie as blossom

Tennis is as boring as running a marathon
I do not adore beans because they are gooey
And that makes me sick
I adore tiring tennis
I appreciate a decent computer.

Maha Bataweel (8)
Cheetham Community Primary School

A Poem About Being An Animal

If you want to be a fast animal,
You should be a cheetah.
If you want to be a small animal,
You should be a mouse.
Being an animal is such fun,
You'll have a great time and be done.
You'll be fast, you'll be good,
You'll be better than wood.

You can be massive, you can be tiny,
You can look like anything, including being shiny.
If you are an animal, you can do anything,
You can eat anything, that is anything.
You can be nice to anyone,
You can be nasty to anyone.

Sara Ahmed (9)
Cheetham Community Primary School

Rich Rameesha

Although I run speedily
As well as that I like walking
An important thing is
I'm as rich as a beautiful, charming queen
Although my mum is pretty
She still cooks deliciously
My dad is helpful like me
My friend, Ammarah, is as beautiful as a butterfly
I like reading like a reader.

Rameesha Khan (8)
Cheetham Community Primary School

Big Ted

Big Ted is fun to have around
He's a really big-hearted bear
I've loved him ever since the day
Dad won him at the fair.

If I bump big Ted down the stairs
He never seems to worry
He doesn't complain or make a fuss
Or tell me I'll be sorry.

The smile upon his face
Never seems to disappear
He didn't even frown or wince
When Mum re-stitched his ear.

Big Ted worries about me
When I am at school each day
Will I dress up warm enough
When I'm sent out to play?

He mothers me when Mum's not there
He understands when I'm sad
He's never grumpy or sharp with me
And nothing makes him mad.

I'm almost as tall as him now
But no matter how much I grow
Big Ted is special to me
And always will be.

Roheen Nawaz (10)
Cheetham Community Primary School

Friendship

Friends, friends, friends,
Friends are friends,
Because they are nice,
Friends are friends,
Because they are kind
Friends are friends,
Because they share
Friends are friends,
Because they care.

Abda Hussain (10)
Cheetham Community Primary School

Trees

A little poem to say thank you to the trees:

Some trees are large
Some trees are small
Some tress grow on walls
Trees give us apples
And rubber and books
All trees are lovely
Whatever their looks.

Tia Rigg & Zara Shazad (9)
Cheetham Community Primary School

Fear

Fear is as black as the night
It smells musty and damp
It tastes like cold Brussels sprouts
It sounds like a loud screeching noise
It feels like a sharp knife
It lives in your bedroom closet.

Lucas Grundy (9)
Holy Family RC Primary School

Pride

Pride is pale blue
It smells like the scent of a ruby-red silky rose
Glistening in the light
It tastes like a soft, squishy white marshmallow
Dipping in a warm, melted chocolate fountain
It sounds like the heavy rain against your window
Going *pitter-patter, pitter-patter*
It feels like a warm, knitted scarf
Against your skin
It lives in the heart of everyone in the world.

Nina Kemp (9)
Holy Family RC Primary School

Happiness

Happiness is red
It smells like blooming flowers
It tastes like candyfloss, fluffy with sugar
It sounds like a harp playing softly
In the dead of night
It feels like a petal floating gently
On the surface of the water
It lives in my house
At least it tries to!

Sophie Castle (9)
Holy Family RC Primary School

Love

Love is pinky-red
It smells like a field of ruby-red roses
It tastes like sweet strawberry milkshake
It sounds like lovebirds cheeping
It feels like a cat's fur
It lives in the tips of angels' wings.

Katie Price (9)
Holy Family RC Primary School

Love

Love is like Cupid's arrow soaring through
The bright, blue, cloudless sky
It smells like pearly pink tulips
Swaying in a bed of ruby red roses
It tastes like glossy, gleaming strawberries
With a glistening glass of sparkling champagne
It sounds like a newborn bird tweeting in a nest
Of freshly-mown grass filled with its mother's scent
It feels like a baby's hand
Stroking its mother's smiling cheek
It lives in the middle of the bright, golden sun.

Georgina Raynor (10)
Holy Family RC Primary School

Love

Love is sapphire blue
It smells of beautiful blossoms blooming under the golden sun
It tastes like sweet, sugary strawberries
It sounds like a harp playing softly under the moonlit sky
It feels like the soft, velvety wings of a gentle butterfly
It lives in the heart of an angel.

Annamay Collier (9)
Holy Family RC Primary School

Depression

Depression is black
It smells like a musty underground car park
It tastes like a soured vinegar shot
It sounds like a storm on your doorstep
It feels like being trapped in a cold mortuary
It lives in the beginning of the end!

Olivia Sullivan (9)
Holy Family RC Primary School

Love

Love is bright red like a cherry tomato
It smells like sweet apples lying in the sun
It tastes like strawberries dipped in a runny chocolate sauce
It sounds like bundles of laughter in a joyful home
It feels like candyfloss clouds floating in the vast blue sky
It lives in the heart of God.

Sarah Bethel (10)
Holy Family RC Primary School

Love

Love is scarlet red
It smells like a field of roses
It tastes like strawberries on a midsummer's day
It sounds like a harp in the middle of a pitch-black night
It feels like a silky petal in the middle of spring
It lives in our hearts.

Rebecca Gainer (9)
Holy Family RC Primary School

Love

Love is a beautiful ruby-red
It smells like a bunch of roses in summer
It tastes like a bundle of crunchy chocolates
It sounds like a bird tweeting at the start of spring
It feels like a soft, gentle bunny hopping around
It lives at the top of your heart.

Jessica Sackfield (9)
Holy Family RC Primary School

Beauty

Beauty is blossom pink
It smells of a field of red roses standing up high
It sounds like a harp playing on calm nights
It tastes like a chocolate cake fresh from the cake shop
It feels like a newborn kitten's fur
It lives in the heart of an angel.

Jade Smith (9)
Holy Family RC Primary School

Love

Love is sparkly pink
It smells like chocolate melting away in the shining sun
It tastes like freshly-made candyfloss
It sounds like birds cheeping sweetly in the pale blue sky
It feels like a fluffy cloud
It lives in a ray of light coming from the sun.

Maissie Lever (9)
Holy Family RC Primary School

Fog

Fog travelled
Into the silent town
Blinding everything it saw
Fog scampered, spreading an immense blanket
But never freed its jaw

Fog grew
Through the clammy forest
Everything becoming doleful
Grasping at every stick and stone
And then drove on.

Hafsa Fahim (10)
Manchester Muslim Prep School

Sam Scared

Scared of bears, scared of a fierce lion
Scared of nits, scared of steam from an iron
Scared of words, scared of baboons
Scared of noon, scared of the light from the moon
Scared of boys, scared of the dark
Scared of girls scared of the park
Scared of Indians, scared of the computer called Dell
Scared of Rob n Hood, scared of the bell
Scared of eagles, scared of fishes
Scared of nuts, scared of dishes
Scared of rats, scared of dying
Scared of skeletons, scared of flying
Scared of nouns, scared of crying
Scared of night, scared of flying
Scared of pots, scared of linking up
Scared of birds, scared of tidying up.

Khaleel Hasnain Ahmed (8)
Manchester Muslim Prep School

Sophie Scared

Sophie scarec of saying hello
Sophie scared of making a little bellow
Sophie scared of an adder
Sophie scared of a ladder
Sophie scared of a sheep that goes *baa!*
Sophie scared of a baby that goes *waa!*
Sophie scared of rain
Sophie scared of a drain
Sophie scared of a girl
Sophie scared of a big whirl
Sophie scared of a bite
Sophie scared of a kite.

Maryam Ajaz (8)
Manchester Muslim Prep School

Our Planets

They are as red as blood,
They are as black as holes,
They are as blue as balls,
They are as orange as folders,
They are as purple as bumpy berries,
They are as turquoise as colourful rainbows,
They are as yellow as the shining sun,
They are as white as the round moon,
They are as bright as a beam of light.

Ibrahim Ali Zulfiqar (8)
Manchester Muslim Prep School

My Little Sister Is . . .

As friendly as a flower
As likeable as a lily
As polite as a pillow
As nice as a nap
As clever as clover
But sometimes . . .
As bossy as a banana
And as silly as a sock.

Abu Bakr Esmail (8)
Manchester Muslim Prep School

A Lonely Scorpion Laying In The Desert Waiting For Its Prey

Not moving an inch,
Waiting for a passing bug,
Still as a statue,
Saw moving insects to catch,
Killing one to eat for food.

Baasim Salam (8)
Manchester Muslim Prep School

On And On

I went to the shop
And bought a uniform,
I went on and on
And bought a toy unicorn.

I went to the shop
And bought a ring,
I went on and on
And bought a bell that goes *ting!*

I went to the shop
And bought a Spanish dress,
I went on and on
And on the floor was a mess.

I went to the shop
And bought a cake,
I went on and on
And bought a rake.

Zainab Rathur (9)
Manchester Muslim Prep School

Our Playground

P laying children
L aughing about
A ngry teachers
Y ou'd think our playground's mad
G angs that children make
R ioting prefects
O utside the gate, parents wait
U nder umbrellas if it rains
N aughty boys fighting
D ogs barking outside the gate.

Haleemah Tayyab (9)
Manchester Muslim Prep School

Fog

Fog is grey, sad and lonely
Fog has no friends
It comes round most bends.

Fog comes in one season
There must be a reason
Fog makes you shiver
Fog makes you quiver.

Fog smokes like an addicted smoker
It smokes in the air
Like it doesn't care.

Quickly the days go by
And warmth kills the fog
And it soon fades away.

Sumaiyah Mahmoud (10)
Manchester Muslim Prep School

Fog

Fog wraps around you,
Blinding you,
You are surrounded by gloomy, dull fog,
It sends a shiver wherever it goes.

The fog is a grey mist,
Also powerful and dark,
The fog creates murder,
It makes you feel as if death has awoken.

The fog spreads itself in every corner,
Making you feel more scared.

Aamna Mohammed (10)
Manchester Muslim Prep School

Milly Moans . . .

Milly moans about her books,
Moans about her pretty looks,
Moans about her long ladder,
Moans about her pink pet adder,
Moans about her classmates,
Moans about her home-made cakes,
Moans about the heavy rain,
Moans about her no-good brain,
Moans about naughty girls,
Moans about wanting pearls.

Dana Ahmed Samatar (8)
Manchester Muslim Prep School

Tom's Scared

Tom's scared of his ladder
Tom's scared of his adder
Tom's scared of running near seas
Tom's scared of running near bees
Tom's scared of sharks
Tom's scared of dog barks
Tom's scared of slaps
Tom's scared of naps.

Hamza Imraan (8)
Manchester Muslim Prep School

Our Class Is . . .

As good as gold
As bad as wild animals
As kind as kittens
As quiet as a library
As helpful as a caretaker
As noisy as a zoo!

Nimrah Razaq (8)
Manchester Muslim Prep School

Helpful Harry

Helpful Harry picks up a cloth
Helpful Harry picks up the socks
Helpful Harry does the washing up
Helpful Harry cleans every cup
Helpful Harry tidies his room
Helpful Harry does it very soon
Helpful Harry puts the socks in the washing machine
Helpful Harry takes them out and they're very clean
Helpful Harry does the beds
Helpful Harry does every one, including Ned's!

Seher Saleem (8)
Manchester Muslim Prep School

Playground Games

P eople screaming like hyenas
L egs are kicking about
A pples are eaten away
Y ellow is the colour of faces
G rand people coming to the playground
R ound and round people go
O ut the mud, the teachers say
U tter silence, teachers say
N o more kicking, dinner ladies say
D on't play in the mud, get out!

Mohamed Kasim Mohamed (8)
Manchester Muslim Prep School

Fog

Fog covers you with its large cloak
Fog swallows everything it can find
Fog annoys people
Fog makes you feel cold
Fog enjoys swallowing.

Aiman Ahmed (10)
Manchester Muslim Prep School

Holly Happy

Holly Happy loves the dark
Happy of rats and dogs that bark
Happy of her fat dad and happy of her mother
Happy of her sis and her tattooed brother
Happy of tall girls, happy of boys
Happy of ghosts and sudden noise
Happy of spiders, happy of bees
Happy of standing under trees
Happy of shadows, happy of adders
Happy of devils, happy of ladders
Happy of hailstones, happy of rain
Happy of falling down a drain
Holly Happy, happy of showing
She's so happy people knowing.

Hanaan Ahmed (9)
Manchester Muslim Prep School

Fog

Fog crept around the street,
He smoked across the land,
He smears his coat across the beach,
He takes over the sea and land.

Fog shows off his ability,
He swallows what we can see,
He leaves in return,
An area very misty.

Fog works hard,
He works for a couple of hours,
Fog starts to feel drowsy,
He has got too tired to carry on.

Mariyah Nadeem (10)
Manchester Muslim Prep School

My Cat Is . . .

As beautiful as a prince
As handsome as anyone's face
As furry as a poodle
As adorable as a dog
As playful as any other cat
As fast as an earthquake's cracks splitting
As sparkling eyes as a gush of water from a clear spring
As cute as a kitten
As fit as a fiddle
As clean as any other cat
He is so clean, cleaner than any human.

Hanna Imraan (8)
Manchester Muslim Prep School

Autumn

The yellow-brown leaves
Twisting around
Coming nearer and nearer to the ground.

Big gold leaves swinging
Down from the trees
Squirrels live in the trees, eating acorns.

Abdullah Khan (7)
Manchester Muslim Prep School

Our Class Is . . .

As good as gold
As bad as a rhino
As kind as a mother
As quiet as a mouse
As helpful as a teacher
As noisy as a dragon.

Mustafa Estwani (8)
Manchester Muslim Prep School

Fog

Fog is like smoke
Fog takes away your sight
Fog never spoke
Fog started in the night.

Fog spread everywhere
Fog hadn't a single care
Fog spread its cloak
Fog, he never spoke.

Fog is grey and black
He will come
It's like you're in a sack
Fog starts to hum.

Fog is cold
Fog is bold
Fog is gone
Fog, there is none.

Aneesa Tahir Malik (10)
Manchester Muslim Prep School

Fog!

Fog scatters smoke everywhere
Fog breathes a cold breeze on you
Fog covers anything you see

Fog is a blind season
Fog is very cloudy
Fog is miserable

Fog is crying
Fog is a dull colour
Fog is never happy.

Haleemah Hassan (10)
Manchester Muslim Prep School

Autumn Is Here

Gold, scarlet and brown,
Orange leaves weaving down.

Children wearing coats and hats,
People warming up on mats.

Berries fall on the ground,
Leaves twist all around.

Squirrels searching,
For berries and nuts to eat.

Children gathering leaves,
In a pile.

Hedgehogs eating
And searching for somewhere to sleep.

Amirah Mohammed (7)
Manchester Muslim Prep School

Fog

Fog is dark
Fog is dull
Fog is misty
Fog is gloomy.

Fog exhales smoke
Fog surrounds you like gas
Fog prowled to every street corner.

Fog is baffling and weird
Fog is horribly mean
Fog is powerful, that no one can stop
Fog is dangerous!

Harris Zafar (10)
Manchester Muslim Prep School

Fog

Dark, dull fog, it's out there
And I'm really scared stiff because . . .
Fog is insane, I know myself,
That fog is as mad as a hatter.

Fog loves manslaughter,
Which means it enjoys killing,
It makes us feel uneasy,
Fog is too strong for us.

Fog spreads its cruelty everywhere,
Fog loses very seldom,
It can take over the most powerful soldier,
It swallows all in its path.

Fog takes a deep breath,
Then smokes a dozen packets of cigarettes,
Fog enjoys itself a lot
It's killing, smoking and blinding.

It's so strong,
The only way to survive,
Is to stay inside,
Another world.

Nazish Nadeem (10)
Manchester Muslim Prep School

Fog

Fog prowls everywhere
Fog spreads its gigantic cloak
All around the ground
Fog exhales smoke everywhere.

Fog's not opaque and isn't transparent
Fog surrounds you all the time
Fog gobbles up everything in its path
Fog is misty and gloomy, so beware!
It is dangerous!

Bahadur Khan Wasim (10)
Manchester Muslim Prep School

Fog

Fog unfolds his huge, dull, grey blanket over us
Fog exhales in every street corner
Fog engulfs ships at the anchorage
Fog blinds car drivers on the road.

Fog dances and twirls around sorrowfully
Fog brings boredom to children
Fog dresses like Dracula
Fog intimidates everyone
Fog's end is very, very close.

Sumaiyah Mohammed (10)
Manchester Muslim Prep School

Fog

Fog surrounds everything
It swallows everyone
Fog is horribly mean
Powerful fog, nobody can stop him.

Fog is opaque
He blinds you so you can't see
He smokes a lot
And is mean
Fog can make you very blue.

Hiba Raza (10)
Manchester Muslim Prep School

Autumn

Leaves gold, yellow, brown and red
Leaves fall to the ground
The wind blows them slowly down
The hedgehog is finding a place to sleep
For the autumn and winter.

Adil Ehsan (7)
Manchester Muslim Prep School

Autumn

In autumn hedgehogs hibernate,
In autumn birds migrate.
Gold, red, yellow or brown,
I see leaves falling down.
Children making piles of leaves
And the leaves are from the conker trees.
Squirrels scampering with food to find,
Trying to find the very best kind.
Leaves, leaves, they fall down,
The children push them, conkers are found.
When I see conkers I hear children,
Trying to find the ones that aren't broken.

Aysha Nadeem (10)
Manchester Muslim Prep School

Autumn

Squirrels sprinting across the trees
Little birds picking leaves
Leaves falling to the ground
Helicopters spinning round and round
Berries falling to the ground
Birds taking them as soon as they're found.

Umar Rashid (7)
Manchester Muslim Prep School

Autumn

The brown leaves floating down as the wind blows
The hedgehog running around to find some food
The orange leaves spinning down as the wind blows down
The gold leaves turning down as the wind blows very hard
The red leaves curving down as the wind blows hard.

Bilal Ahmed (7)
Manchester Muslim Prep School

Here Is Autumn

In autumn the leaves fall off the trees
The colour of the leaves are gold, brown and scarlet.

In autumn the leaves flutter, twirl and twist
Off the trees to the ground.

In autumn squirrels run to find their food
Hedgehogs curl up under leaves to go to bed.

In autumn the tall trees are bare
And the birds tweet and they hunt all morning for food.

Saarah Choudary (7)
Manchester Muslim Prep School

Autumn Is Here

Gold, scarlet, crimson and brown
The leaves are everywhere, they are spinning to the ground.
Squirrels move from tree to tree to collect their nuts
So they don't have to collect them in winter.
The hedgehog finds its home in autumn
And sleeps in it for five months.
Birds migrate from Manchester to Africa in autumn
So they can stay somewhere warm.

Eesa Tayyab (7)
Manchester Muslim Prep School

Autumn

The lovely golden-yellow leaves
Swing down the pretty trees.

Yellow, gold, red and brown
Slowly the leaves fall down.

The wind's blowing the leaves
From the old trees.

Abdul Muizz Gaddah (7)
Manchester Muslim Prep School

Autumn

All the leaves are falling down from the trees
They are gold, red, yellow, orange
And the hedgehogs are out and about
As they eat the yummy food.

The rain is falling down
And all the animals are home in bed
All the people are going home
Shops are closed.

Hamza Haq (7)
Manchester Muslim Prep School

Here's Autumn

Yellow, red, orange and brown
And the leaves are flowing down to the ground
Squirrels climbing up the trees
Jumping up and down.

The hedgehog is running
Down the garden to find a home
Squirrel is climbing up a tree
To find some food he can eat.

Maliha Ahmed (7)
Manchester Muslim Prep School

Autumn

Red, orange, yellow and brown leaves
Fluttering on my head and on the ground
Birds migrating and hedgehogs hibernating
Children collecting leaves and conkers
Squirrels collecting nuts for winter
Autumn hi-hi! Summer bye-bye!

Alani Batrisyia Anazim (7)
Manchester Muslim Prep School

Autumn

Hedgehogs are hibernating
And geese are migrating.
Gold, red and yellow leaves
Sycamore keys twist off trees.
In autumn it is cold like the North Pole
And every mole is in its hole.
Squirrels climbing up trees
And jumping over leaves.

Faiz Mohammed (7)
Manchester Muslim Prep School

Autumn

Gold, crimson, yellow and brown
There go the leaves, falling to the ground.
Can you see the birds going to migrate?
There goes the hedgehog, off to hibernate.
Leaves fall to the ground
As they twirl round and round.
There go the leaves twirling
Soon they might start swirling.

Aqsa Saied (7)
Manchester Muslim Prep School

Autumn

Squirrels scuttling all around,
Birds picking berries that fall on the ground.
Gold, red, yellow and brown,
Hear the leaves falling down.
Hedgehogs finding a warm home,
Staying there in winter, all alone.

Zainab Ahmed (8)
Manchester Muslim Prep School

Autumn Leaves

Autumn is here
The squirrels are scampering
Looking for food.

The brown leaves are falling
Onto the ground
The hedgehog is saying, 'Sleep tight!'

The leaves are changing colour
Red and orange and brown.

All the animals say, 'Goodnight!'
All the leaves are rushing
Goodnight!

Yusuf Mahmoud (7)
Manchester Muslim Prep School

Autumn Has Arrived

Gold, red and brown leaves
Flutter down to the ground.

The prickly hedgehog
Trying to look for a home to hibernate in.

The children putting on
Their woolly clothes.

Squirrels go back in trees
To take their deep sleep.

Faris Akhtar (7)
Manchester Muslim Prep School

Autumn

Yellow, red, orange and brown
The leaves go down.

In autumn the leaves fall down
Slowly they go round.

The leaves go down
Onto the ground.

The hedgehog sleeps at night
And looks at the light.

Haashim Ahmed (7)
Manchester Muslim Prep School

Autumn

Hello autumn,
Crimson-red, yellow and brown
I can see leaves swirling down.

Moles in their holes
Hedgehogs who hibernate,
Squirrels collecting nuts
Birds who migrate.

As the wind weaves
It's time to clear up the leaves.

Amaani Esmail (7)
Manchester Muslim Prep School

Autumn

Brown, crimson, gold, orange and yellow
Leaves twisting, swerving slowly down
The hedgehog finding a cosy home
With the leaves that have been blown off the trees
The squirrels scampering around
Searching for berries, acorns and nuts to eat
People looking for gold, scarlet, and brown leaves
To make big piles
The sycamore keys spinning away
Landing on the school playground
The birds tweeting as the yellow, brown and red leaves fall.

Seif Mohammed (8)
Manchester Muslim Prep School

Autumn

Squirrels climbing up the trees
Trying to find some nuts
Hedgehogs in a pile of leaves
Making a warm bed to sleep.

Red, brown, yellow and orange leaves
Floating and swirling from the trees
The wind is blowing the leaves
The leaves are rustling on the trees.

Amera Hussain (7)
Manchester Muslim Prep School

Autumn

Orange, yellow, scarlet and brown,
Leaves are spinning and falling.
Squirrels climbing trees
And running across the ground.
In autumn it is cold and windy,
Moles, badgers, hedgehogs
And squirrels in hibernation.
Swallows are migrating,
Flying all the way to Africa.

Talha Khan (8)
Manchester Muslim Prep School

Dreams

Dreams, dreams, everywhere
Dreams, dreams, they're really fair
Dreams, dreams, everywhere
Dreams, dreams, always there
Dreams, dreams, get your own way
Dreams, dreams, get up and fly away!

Joshua Flynn (10)
St Charles' RC Primary School, Swinton

Love

Love is red like roses
It tastes like strawberries
It smells like perfume
It looks like a big love heart
It sounds like tweeting birds
It feels like a new beginning.

Louise Hawkens (8)
St Charles' RC Primary School, Swinton

Indie

Looking through the window,
I could see her big brown eyes,
All she wants to do is play by my side.
She sees a cat run across the grass
And all she does is scratch the glass.
Up and down the stairs she runs,
To see us kids having fun.
My mum says, 'Let her out!'
And all she does is jump about.
She plays with me and my friends,
But then it gets dark and the games end.
She runs to the tap on the side of our house,
With her tongue flopping right out,
She drinks the water, then lies on the floor,
You can see in her eyes she wants some more.
Come on, Indie, we have to go in,
Or Mum will put your tea in the bin!
Off she walks and eats her tea,
Then I wrap her up cosy, just like me.
My dog Indie is the best
And now she is sleeping, having a rest.

Brittany Lowe (10)
St Charles' RC Primary School, Swinton

Life

When I'm older I want to go to Mars
And sail across the stars,
When I come back to Earth,
I want to make a family birth.

Son, daughter, same to me,
If none, I'll start a new family.
I had a loss, it was my wife,
I wish I had her still in my life.

Joe Gorman (11)
St Charles' RC Primary School, Swinton

Queen Victoria

Born in Kensington Palace,
Had nine children, one called Alice.
Drawing and painting was her thing,
Sometimes she also liked to sing.
She kept a diary every day,
Became queen at 18, but found time to play!
With all nine children and a good wife to be,
To her husband, Prince Albert, who to her heart had the key.
So devastated was she when he died,
Behind black clothing every day she did hide.
There were seven attempts in all to kill her,
But she reigned for a record 64 years, a winner!
She awarded the brave with the Victoria Cross,
Usually when for their country, their life they had lost.
First to Charles Lucas, but since have been more,
Caring for her subjects wasn't a chore!
A long and hard life, but worthwhile she knew,
She joined her dear Albert and died at 82!

Helen Morley (10)
St Charles' RC Primary School, Swinton

Everything

Dreams, dreams, everywhere,
Dreams, dreams, sometimes tear.
Fear, fear, in your heart,
Fear, fear, like a dart.
Change, change, somewhere new,
Change, change, who are you?

Some things are right and some things are wrong,
Some things are short and some things are long,
Some things are small and some things are tall,
Everything is different overall.

Kieron Robert Fawcett (10)
St Charles' RC Primary School, Swinton

Growing Up

Summer's morning, ready for school,
Will other people think that I'm cool?
This is the question I worry about,
I think about it always, without a doubt.

Through the gates, here I come,
School get ready, I'm not dumb.
Separated from my friends, oh, what a shame,
No one to talk to, this is such a pain!

Hurrying to my classroom, don't want to be late,
Suddenly, a girl comes up to me and asks if I want to be her mate!
I decided she was nice enough, so I said yes,
Then I scored full marks in class, no more, no less.

Finally it's dinner time, only half a day to go,
Then the cook asked me if I wanted sprouts, but obviously I said no!
Before I knew it, the day was over,
Now we have homework, Sir is such a loader.

Walking home, very stressed out,
Better get my homework done, without a doubt.
Wish I could just go out and play,
But that definitely won't happen, seeing as it's just my first day.

Katherine Shanley (10)
St Charles' RC Primary School, Swinton

Growing Up

G radually, as I get older
R eception through to juniors, now I have to use a folder
O ff to high school we go
W e have to take it with the flow
 I CT, art, English, science, history and maths
N ow with my new friends we have some laughs
G reat time I've had today

U sually we always say
P lease, let's hope we don't get homework today!

Daniel Moore (10)
St Charles' RC Primary School, Swinton

Colours Of The Rainbow

What is red?
A rose is red with a gorgeous smell.
What is yellow?
The sun is yellow with a radiant gleam.
What is pink?
Blossom is pink with a pretty, delicate scent.
What is green?
The grass is green with a lovely, fresh, heady smell.
What is orange?
The sunset is orange, with a spectacular radiant shine.
What is purple?
My scarf is purple with a scrumptious fluffy touch.
What is blue?
The sky is blue with its breathtaking colour lifting up to Heaven.

Laura Woodward (9)
St Charles' RC Primary School, Swinton

What I Want To Be!

Footballer I want to be,
But we will have to wait and see,
I do have the talent, skill and pace,
But it's if I want to win that race.

It's not the money or the fame that attracts me,
It's the love of the game that does it for me,
The speed and the thrill,
To the tricks and the skill.

Work hard at school,
Eat healthy gruel,
Look after little old me,
If a footballer I want to be!

Shaun Taylor-Whitfield (11)
St Charles' RC Primary School, Swinton

Animal Crackers

Snakes go hiss,
Crocs go snap,
As they sneak up,
Behind your back!

The lion's mighty roar
And the mouse's tiny squeak,
This is the way
The animals speak!

Birds in the sky,
Fish in the sea,
Living alongside,
You and me.

Living together,
Sharing our space,
The world is more than
Just the human race!

Natasha Martland (9)
St Charles' RC Primary School, Swinton

Blackpool

I went to Blackpool,
That was after school.

It was really exciting,
Except my dad started fighting.

When he stopped,
He really hopped,
Because of his bad leg.

And that was the story
About me at Blackpool.

Ryan McGuinness (10)
St Charles' RC Primary School, Swinton

My First Day

I'm lost in the corridor,
No one there.
I can't believe I'm doing this,
It's so not fair.
I can't find my way,
The world encloses me,
What can I do?
I so want to be free.
I wander around,
Still no help in sight,
Come on, get yourself together,
Put up a fight.
I open the door,
There is a sudden stare,
Like I said before,
It's so not fair!

Gemma Johns (10)
St Charles' RC Primary School, Swinton

My First Lunchtime

I want to see my mummy
Because I have a painful tummy

I want to see my mummy
So I get my dinner money

I want to see my mummy
So I get a chummy

I want to see my mummy
But not until ten-past three
That's quite enough for a big boy like me!

Deklan Cusick (10)
St Charles' RC Primary School, Swinton

Caterpillar And Butterfly

Caterpillar, caterpillar go so slow
Caterpillar, caterpillar watch how they go
Caterpillar, caterpillar grow some wings
Caterpillar, caterpillar comes out in spring

Butterfly, butterfly fly so high
Butterfly, butterfly touch the sky
Butterfly, butterfly land on a branch
Butterfly, butterfly watch how they dance.

Jason Lineker (10)
St Charles' RC Primary School, Swinton

Times Tables And Homework

Times tables and homework
Are all the same things,
I just wish my mind
Would go *ding-ding,*
Times tables are hard,
Homework is barred,
Times tables and homework
Are all the same things.

Molly Frattasi (10)
St Charles' RC Primary School, Swinton

Loneliness

Loneliness is the colour blue
It tastes like coffee without any cream
It smells like rotten cabbage, not very nice indeed
Loneliness looks like rain dripping from a lonely cloud in the sky
Loneliness sounds like a sad cat miaowing sadly
Loneliness feels like an empty bucket.

Juliette Graham (7)
St Charles' RC Primary School, Swinton

Camping

I find camping really great,
It seems impossible to actually hate.

Lying down in the twilight,
Watching sparrows in their flight.

This is where I like my time spent,
At night sleeping in our cosy tent.

When I wake up ready to run,
I had some more great fun.

Then the time came, I was ready to go,
I was happy, because I knew I'd come again though.

Joel Healey (10)
St Charles' RC Primary School, Swinton

Inside And Outside

Outside we play together
Playing, jumping, hopping, singing, dancing,
So let's get playing!

Inside we work together,
Learn, think, speak, draw, count, write, share,
School is cool inside and outside!

Beth Renshaw (7)
St Charles' RC Primary School, Swinton

Love

Love is red
It tastes like juicy strawberries
And smells like wild flowers on a nice, sunny day
It looks like a big, red, love heart
Love sounds like happy music
And feels like a soft breeze.

Finlay Cox (7)
St Charles' RC Primary School, Swinton

My Poem

Writing poems is very hard,
For I am certainly no bard!
I tried to ask my mum for help,
But she said, 'Go and do it yourself!'

So I went to ask my brother,
But he said, 'Tough, find another!'
Next I went to my stepdad,
But all his ideas were really bad!

Then I decided to ask my nan,
But she was busy with the frying pan!
Even my friend, who lives next door,
Couldn't help me anymore!

So, that only left the cat,
Who wouldn't speak, so that was that!
That's my story, loud and clear,
I definitely won't win a prize - oh dear!

Joseph McMullen (10)
St Charles' RC Primary School, Swinton

High School!

Am I excited? Am I in shock?
How has time gone this fast?
Tick-tock, tick-tock.

I am walking through the gates now
I am starting to panic
Where are my mates?

I walk in the school
I am shaking like mad
I feel like a fool.

Is this right?
Am I here?
This is going to be a really hard year!

Nicole Greenhalgh (11)
St Charles' RC Primary School, Swinton

School

People say that school is fun,
But I regard that last bit as a pun.
You have to be there by the crack of dawn,
All sat at tables, stifling a yawn.

Geography, history, English, maths,
They really don't raise many laughs.
The teachers try, they surely do,
But some children just don't want to.

Whenever I sneeze I bang my knees,
Under the very low table.
Bell rings, it's dinner time, we all gather
To be fed by our cook, Mabel.

Yippee! It's PE!
This is our favourite subject.
Football, netball, rounders too,
We get in teams, then check what we have to do.

Burning off energy, the ball's being tapped,
They say fresh air is good for you,
But we are all zapped,
Now they expect us to go and do maths!

Ding-ding, the bells ring,
We're free to go, you hear us all sing.
That's it for another day,
See you all tomorrow, we hope anyway.

Matthew Smith (9)
St Charles' RC Primary School, Swinton

Little Bird

I wish I were a little bird,
With great, enormous wings,
I would fly around this lovely world,
To look at all the things.

Emily Naylor (7)
St Charles' RC Primary School, Swinton

Trees

Trees in winter stand so strong,
With their branches stretched out long,
Then the snow falls from the sky,
Lying on the branches high.

Then on the trees the buds appear,
Telling us that spring is here,
Birds sit singing in the trees,
Feathers blowing in the breeze.

Then the leaves start to appear,
Showing us that summer's near,
The blossoms all begin to bloom,
But autumn will be here real soon.

Then the leaves start to fall down,
Fluttering by us to the ground,
Changing colours to red and gold,
Soon it's going to be cold.

Jazmine Barker (9)
St Charles' RC Primary School, Swinton

It's A Sport Thing

Tennis, soccer,
Cricket, basketball,
Remember to lock the locker,
Don't give your girlfriend a call,
Smell of sweat,
Man of the match,
When I'm rich,
I'm gonna buy a jet,
Have a rest,
Sport's the best!

Sebastian Ward-Bowmer (10)
St Charles' RC Primary School, Swinton

My Name

I am Abs, that's my name,
Any day you want, I can play your game,
Monday to Sunday, all the hours,
Any week, any year,
I am free all the time,
Just shout my name and I'll be round,
I am Abs, that's my name,
Any day you want, I can play your game,
Dude!

Abigail Hamer (9)
St Charles' RC Primary School, Swinton

Love!

Love is bright orange
Tastes of freshly baked cake
Love is the smell of garlic bread
It looks like my beautiful rabbit, Sunshine
Sounds like running water
Love is happy and warm!

Matthew Hope (7)
St Charles' RC Primary School, Swinton

Anger!

Anger is pitch-black
And it tastes like a mouldy plum
It smells like dog muck
It looks like prison
And sounds like a dog barking
Anger hates me!

Charlie Beth Parker (7)
St Charles' RC Primary School, Swinton

High School

On my first day, it's such a fright,
Lots of homework every night.
The headmaster takes us to our places,
Lots of school ties, blazers and laces.
Fairy cakes, chocolate cakes and lots of buns
And even some of the schoolwork is lots of fun.
Sometimes we make home-made bread,
But also I had to sharpen my pencil lead.
Finally, I get my own way,
Can't wait for another day!

Emma Mollard (10)
St Charles' RC Primary School, Swinton

Love!

Love is as red as the sun rising
It tastes like Cadbury's Caramel chocolate
It smells like sweet perfume
It looks like a beating heart
It sounds like you and your family playing happily
It feels like being warm and cosy in your home.

Lauren Ainscough (8)
St Charles' RC Primary School, Swinton

Rage

Rage is red like a bubbling volcano
It tastes like hot chilli peppers burning your tongue
It smells like molten rock
It looks like a burning car
It sounds like crackling fireworks
It feels hot and uncontrollable.

Olivia Adelaide Myrtle (9)
St Charles' RC Primary School, Swinton

I Can't Find My Friends

I can't find my friends today,
I've looked everywhere,
In five cupboards,
In the classroom
And in the hall
And in the headteacher's office,
I got told off and had to miss my break,
They were behind me all the time!

Robert Barton (8)
St Charles' RC Primary School, Swinton

Football

F ast and furious
O h no
O wn goal
T ackle and recover the ball
B rake and pass to the
A ttacker
L ong ball delivered
L ow ball across the face of the goal . . . *goal!*

Harry Warburton (9)
St Charles' RC Primary School, Swinton

Happiness

Happiness is yellow like the warm sunshine
It tastes like some ripe bananas
It smells like thick, warm custard and flowers
It looks like a warm day
It sounds like happy children playing
It feels like everyone is around you playing with you.

Maisie Cox (8)
St Charles' RC Primary School, Swinton

I'm Gonna Write A Poem

I'm gonna write a poem
I really want to win
When I do this poem
I hope it won't go in the bin.

I'm really very excited
Writing is my pleasure
I hope everyone takes care of it
Like it is a treasure.

I'm gonna write a poem
I really want to win
Oh, I've written my poem
I'd better hand it in!

Kristine Norwood (9)
St Charles' RC Primary School, Swinton

My Friend!

My best friend is pink
Who's your best friend?
My best friend is hot pink,
My best friend is baby pink,
My best friend is sparkly pink,
My best friend is glamorous pink,
My best friend is groovy pink,
I love pink,
Do you like pink?
Pink makes me smile,
Pink is the best!

Chloe Broughall (9)
St Charles' RC Primary School, Swinton

My Friend!

Who is my friend?
My friend is Lucy,
She's funny and silly,
She's great to have for a friend,
She runs like bananas
And looks like an apple
She's very healthy
Can't you see?
She's cherries.

Natalya Cusick (8)
St Charles' RC Primary School, Swinton

Anger

Anger is bright red
It tastes like a bitter lemon
It smells like a mouldy sandwich
It looks like a pitch-black stormy sky
It sounds like stamping feet down the stairs
It feels like wet rain, *pitter-patter, pitter-patter.*

Amy Plaister (9)
St Charles' RC Primary School, Swinton

Craziness

Craziness is all different colours
It tastes like custard and jelly
It smells like my dad's belly
It looks like fireworks exploding in the sky
It sounds like *bang! bang!* cheese pie!

Jack Grimes (8)
St Charles' RC Primary School, Swinton

My Friend

Have you got a friend like mine?
Short, brown hair,
Doesn't really care if it's everywhere,
Won't do a dare,
Not naughty,
Uses her mind,
My friend is one of a kind!

Georgia Tandy (8)
St Charles' RC Primary School, Swinton

Happiness

Happiness is red like a heart
It tastes like sweets
It smells lovely and happy
It looks like smiley faces
It sounds like a pocket of laughter
It feels like friends everywhere.

Lukas Copak (8)
St Charles' RC Primary School, Swinton

Love

Love is red
It tastes like strawberry ice cream
It smells like red roses
It looks like a big, juicy strawberry
It sounds like a heart beating
It feels like wet clay on my fingertips.

Melissa Capps (8)
St Charles' RC Primary School, Swinton

I Am Scared

I am scared

There is a huge blue monster,
Who lives under my bed,
I hear his long white teeth click,
He is waiting to be fed.

I am scared

I don't know what to do,
I shiver in my sheets,
I squeeze my eyes shut
And wait till he might just go away.

I am scared

He marches up to me
And pats me on the back,
But then he says the meanest thing,
'Let me in your bed, or I will eat you!'

My mum comes in the room,
And sees him in bed,
She smacks his bottom *hard!*
And then he runs away.

Haniyya Shaikh (9)
St James' CE Primary School, Birch-in-Rusholme

Guess My Animal

Guess my animal

A small animal with a big brain
Not a lonely creature
Technical at building and is good at the game.

Guess my animal

Digging is its mate
Ouch! If it bites you
Growl! It protects you if you're in trouble.

Guess my animal

Can land on its feet from jumping
And moves silently if its hunting
Tricks its prey and eats it with pride.

Harry Joseph Gallagher (9)
St James' CE Primary School, Birch-in-Rusholme

Under The Sea

There is a dizzy, dancing dolphin diving down deep
A marvellous mermaid making mango milkshake
There are fighting fish getting furious about fishing nets.

Under the sea

There is a shivering seahorse smoking seaweed
A creepy-crawly crab craving cranberries
There's a white whale waving its tail in windy weather.

Alice Hare (9)
St James' CE Primary School, Birch-in-Rusholme

My Wishes

My wish would be,
A little sister so I can brush her hair,
£100 to spend on computer games,
Fifty books to read all night.

My wish would be,
A cheeky monkey to be my friend,
An elephant to finish off my drinks,
A giraffe to get my toys off the high shelf.

My wish would be,
A red rocking ruby rumbling,
A sparkling silver star,
A gleaming golden goblet.

Laura Clarke (9)
St James' CE Primary School, Birch-in-Rusholme

Blue Is

Blue is a dolphin
In the sea, leaping
Blue is a swimming pool
Quietly sleeping

Blue is the sea
That's lovely and wet
Blue is a City shirt
That makes you sweat

Blue is the sky
That's big and crowded
Blue is a plaster
So your food doesn't get infected

Blue is some berries
Lovely and juicy
Blue is a ball
Round and bouncy.

Esmé Elizabeth Doolin (8)
St Mary's CE Primary School, Urmston

My Magic Box

(Based on 'Magic Box' by Kit Wright)

I will put in my box . . .

The last smile of my grandad
Monkeys in butterfly suits doing karate
The dreamy smell of a chocolate bath.

I will put in my box . . .
A ginger cat riding a spotty horse
Beach shells covered in hearts, flying over the sea
The last stroke of my beautiful dog.

I will put in my box . . .

The sweet aroma of my grandma's perfume
A frog riding a dolphin across the waves
Flying pizzas with hundreds of pepperoni.

My box is fashioned from . . .

Metal and rich rubies
Crystals for the lid
And funny jokes in the corners
Sharks' teeth for hinges.

I would fly on a magic carpet in my box
Visit the hottest place in the world
Then sunbathe with a hundred cocktails by my side.

Jodie McRoy (9)
Seedley Primary School

My Magic Box

(Based on 'Magic Box' written by Kit Wright)

I will put in my box . . .

A pig and a duck scoring a fabulous goal
A blob of chocolate on top of a volcano
Multicoloured fish in the air, in a circle.

I will put in my box . . .

The dancing of a frog and a human jumping
A piranha sizzling on a hot barbecue
The texture of hugging a tree made out of ice.

I will put in my box . . .

A rose smelling like perfume so sweetly
The bright sunshine speaking a different language
The touch of a toddler smiling.

My box is fashioned from . . .
Carved wood, steel and gold,
With a moon on the lid and chocolate in the corners
Its hinges are the toe of an eagle.

I will fly on a carpet to Egypt in my box
Then wash ashore on the shiny beach
And relax under a chocolate tree.

Bianca Tadete (9)
Seedley Primary School

My Magic Box

(Based on 'Magic Box' by Kit Wright)

I will put in my box . . .

A snail that runs as fast as a cheetah
A kitten roaring as loud as a lion
Some soft chocolate swishing in the blue sea.

I will put in my box . . .

The feel of a furry cat licking my hand
A telephone sandwich, with ketchup
The sun as black as the night sky.

My box is fashioned from . . .

Diamonds, steel and wood with crystals on the lid
And secret things in the corners
Its hinges are made from shark's teeth.

I shall fly in my box over the Atlantic Ocean
And skate down the mountains of ice
Into the sand of the seas.

Sam Curwen (9)
Seedley Primary School

My Magic Box

(Based on 'Magic Box' by Kit Wright)

I will put in my box . . .

A pig as big as the world eating Chelsea FC
The smell of a chicken and mash mountain
With a marshmallow stream
A fish on the moon riding a moon buggy.

I will put in my box . . .

A spider pig, ant and a fly in a band
The sound of waves crashing against the rocks
A dolphin swimming in the forest.

My box is made from . . .

Gold and diamonds
With WWE spinner belts on the lid
And Champions League Cups for hinges.

I will jump from an aeroplane in my box
From 666,666,666 feet in the air
Into the Pacific Ocean and float to the deserts and the pyramids.

Callum James Henderson-Playfair (9)
Seedley Primary School

My Magic Box

(Based on 'Magic Box' by Kit Wright)

I will put in my box . . .

A milk chocolate volcano exploding
With white and hazelnut chocolate
The delicate touch of a tiny baby
And the beautiful aroma of vanilla wafting by.

I will put in my box . . .

A lilac kitten slipping through bronze meadows
The moon and stars from outer space
And the last soft kiss of my nana.

I will put in my box . . .

An attractive fairy riding on a dolphin
A polar bear as white as snow
And a swan on a sapphire lake.

My box is fashioned from . . .

Crystal and silver with rainbows on the lid
And whispers in the corners
The hinges are made of coconut shells.

I will float in my box on the Mediterranean Sea
And wash up on a faraway beach
Surrounded by palm trees and kids' cocktails.

Caitlin Alice Craddock (9)
Seedley Primary School

My Magic Box
(Based on 'Magic Box' by Kit Wright)

I will put in my box . . .

A lilac Pegasus swooping over a crystal lake
White chocolate rain clouds with milk chocolate rain
A baby's faint cry from next door.

I will put in my box . . .

Snowflakes the size of elephants in autumn
A baby-blue pig flying over a purple field
A cat singing 'Hound Dog' by Elvis Presley.

I will put in my box . . .

A delicate rose in a pink sunset
A rainbow sun with milk chocolate rays
The sound of a wave hitting a rock.

My box is fashioned from . . .

Precious sapphires with poppies on the lid
And daisies in the corners
Its hinges are tails of an angelfish.

I shall gallop in my box on a beautiful white horse
And then end up being a professional show jumper
At the Royal Ascot.

Gemma Wagstaffe (10)
Seedley Primary School

The Magic Box

(Based on 'Magic Box' by Kit Wright)

I will put in the box . . .

My mum's creamy mash
The warmth of my brother's love
And the last few cuddles with my pet dog.

I will put in the box . . .

A chocolate town getting eaten bit by bit
Snow falling down in summer
And the crash of one million waves.

I will put in my box . . .

A lion whisperer saying, 'You're my best friend'
The Sydney Harbour Bridge from a great height
And the rattle from a rattlesnake.

My box is fashioned from . . .

Caramel swirls that will never melt with topaz stars on the lid
The corners are soft pink pillows
And its hinges are twisted like a rattlesnake's tail.

I shall fly in my box all around the world
From the Atlantic to China
And arrive home in time for tea.

Chloe Rawlings (9)
Seedley Primary School

My Magic Box

(Based on 'Magic Box' by Kit Wright)

I will put in my box . . .

A green monkey driving a blue Lamborghini
The first smile of a baby and its first word
Lying down in a melted Galaxy.

I will put in my box . . .

A big blue drunken whale running around
The smell of a thousand red roses
Lying down on a fluffy candyfloss bed.

My box is fashioned from . . .
Metal, gold and octopus tentacles on the lid
And magic wishes in the corners
Its hinges are elephant trunks.

I will swim in my box to a magic island
Where I will live, surrounded by trees.

Jordan Egerton (9)
Seedley Primary School

The Funny Face Poem

You!
Your head is like an egg
You!
Your eyes are like marbles
You!
Your ears are like mangos
You!
Your nostrils are like train tunnels
You!
Your nose is like the Eiffel Tower!

Hamza Tahir (8) & Ahsan Mohsin
Temple Primary School

Alphabet Poem

A is for Amy whose jokes are a bore
B is for Becky who's always slamming the door
C is for Cinderella who's always at the ball
D is for Dora who's always in the mall
E is for Emma who's always fussing about others
F is for Fiona who loves her mothers
G is for Gilbert who's covered in slime
H is for Hannah who's never on time
I is for Ikrah who drinks lots of fizzy
J is for Jamie who loves Lizzy
K is for Katie who can't stop eating
L is for Lizzy who can't stop beating
M is for Maddie who can't stop watching movies
N is for Nevra who always boogies
O is for Oliver who teases the cat
P is for Peter whose singing is flat
Q is for Quinn who never says thanks
R is for Raven who plans to rob banks
S is for Sabrina who has a fat belly
T is for Troy who is really smelly
U is for Usman who makes a lot of noise
V is for Violet who bullies the boys
W is for Wajia whose voice is like a bell
X is for Xasim who always tells
Y is for Yasmin who likes wearing ties
Z is for Zoë who never tells lies.

Shamera Ashfaq (8) & Mevish Ahmed
Temple Primary School

Monsters

Monsters are creepy
Monsters are sleepy
Monsters are stinky
Monsters are silky
Monsters are hairy
Monsters are scary
Monsters eat cats
Bats and rats
Monsters are greedy
Monsters are speedy
Monsters are fast
But they're
Always last!

Shoaib Mohammed (8) & Mohammed Hafeez
Temple Primary School

Pyramid Poem

A pyramid is like a witch's hat
A pyramid is made out of sandy stones
A pyramid has many, many secrets
Don't go inside
If you do, the tomb will curse you
Many, many blocks were put on by Egyptian slaves
Some died
Some survived
Some cried
Some were buried alive!

Ifla Araf (8) & Sabah Gohar
Temple Primary School

Young Writers Information

We hope you have enjoyed reading this book - and that you will continue to enjoy it in the coming years.

If you like reading and writing poetry drop us a line, or give us a call, and we'll send you a free information pack.

Alternatively if you would like to order further copies of this book or any of our other titles, then please give us a call or log onto our website at www.youngwriters.co.uk

Young Writers Information
Remus House
Coltsfoot Drive
Peterborough
PE2 9JX

(01733) 890066